1·2·3 Blocks

Beginning Block Activities for Young Children

Written by **Evelyn Petersen, B.S., M.A.**
Illustrated by **Marion Hopping Ekberg**

Totline® Publications
A Division of Frank Schaffer Publications, Inc.
Torrance, California

With appreciation to the Traverse City Cooperative Preschool in Traverse City, Michigan, for photographs of children's block creations that helped inspire this book.

This book is dedicated to all early childhood teachers. I hope that it will help you use the blocks in your center even more effectively to increase children's enjoyment, creativity, and thinking skills. If I could buy only one thing for my classroom, it would be blocks. This book will tell you why.

—E.P.

Totline Publications would like to acknowledge the following child-care professionals for contributing some of the activities in this book: Sarah Cooper, Arlington, TX; Heather Ray, Downington, PA.

Managing Editor: Kathleen Cubley
Editor: Gayle Bittinger
Contributing Editors: Carol Gnojewski, Susan Hodges, Elizabeth McKinnon, Jean Warren
Copyeditor: Kris Fulsaas
Proofreader: Miriam Bulmer
Editorial Assistant: Durby Peterson
Graphic Designer/Layout Artist: Sarah Ness/Gordon Frazier
Graphic Designer (Cover): Brenda Mann Harrison
Production Manager: Melody Olney

ISBN: 1-57029-185-3

Library of Congress Catalog Number 97-62222
Printed in the United States of America
Published by Totline® Publications
Editorial Office: P.O. Box 2250
　　　　　　　　Everett, WA 98203
Business Office: 23740 Hawthorne Blvd.
　　　　　　　　Torrance, CA 90505

20 19 18 17 16 15 14 13 12 11 10 9 8 7 6 5 4 3 2 1

Introduction

Early childhood educators have always emphasized the importance of blocks as a basic, daily learning material for children. Children of all ages love blocks because the possibilities for constructing or creating with them are endless. The opportunities for learning with blocks are equally infinite. When children play with blocks, they learn many kinds of intellectual and social skills, from vocabulary and mathematical thinking to goal setting and cooperation. *1-2-3 Blocks* will give you fresh and interesting ideas for teaching all of these skills, and it will help you make the blocks in your classroom more enjoyable and exciting.

As you look through this book, you will find tips on how to use blocks to challenge your children's thinking and problem-solving skills, increase language and literacy, practice perceptual and memory skills, and nurture creativity. You will learn how to help your children use unit blocks, hollow blocks, and table blocks in new ways, incorporating them into themes and learning games. You will also discover ways to make your own unique blocks and gain ideas for using them with your children.

1-2-3 Blocks is filled with ideas for making block play fun and educational. Enjoy!

Contents

Unit Blocks

Why Use Unit Blocks?

Unit blocks are a wonderful addition to any early childhood classroom. Here are a few reasons why.

- Unit blocks are open-ended materials and nurture creativity in many ways.

- Children of any age or skill level can use unit blocks successfully, because there is no wrong way to build or create with them.

- Unit blocks can be used to increase vocabulary and enhance literacy.

- Unit blocks can be used to teach many math and science skills.

- Perceptual, motor, and memory skills are developed through unit block play.

- Playing with unit blocks increases your children's attention span and level of concentration.

- Playing cooperatively with unit blocks teaches teamwork and responsible social behavior.

- Classroom themes can be integrated into unit block play.

What Are Unit Blocks?

Unit blocks are smooth, unpainted hardwood blocks of various sizes. Unit blocks are precision cut. Each type of block is exactly the same size and weight. The basic unit block is a short rectangle, equal to two square blocks. Two short rectangles (or four squares) equal a double unit or a medium rectangle; four short rectangles (or eight squares) equal a quadruple unit or a long rectangle. Cylinders, ramps, triangles, pillars, arches, and other shapes are also available. Uniformity and precision balance make unit blocks easy for children to use for creating simple to complex constructions.

Where to Use Unit Blocks

There are a few things to keep in mind when designating a unit block play area.

Space—Reserve, if possible, about one-third of your room's floor space for block play. This space can also double as a circle time or large motor area.

Visibility—Make sure the block area is visible from other parts of the room for easy supervision.

Traffic—Keep the block play area out of the main traffic flow so that block construction can continue uninterrupted.

Storage—Have open shelves nearby for easy storage.

Floor—Cover the block play area with a carpet that has a smooth, flat surface, if possible. This will help to reduce the noise of block building, keep the children warm while sitting and working on the floor, and provide a sturdy building surface.

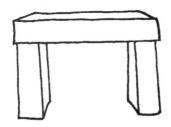

When to Use Unit Blocks

Unit blocks are important for learning and should be available to your children every day during free choice time, if possible.

How Many Do You Need?

For a group of 15 to 20 three- to five-year-olds, you will need a supply of about 300 basic units and cylinders, including extra pieces such as curves, triangles, ramps, and switches. Look for "school" sets, "half sets," or "builder" sets at school supply stores and in school supply catalogs. A set of quality, well-made unit blocks is an investment, but one that will last a lifetime.

Stages of Unit Block Play

When your children play with blocks, they are not just playing, they are thinking and solving problems. From the very first stage of picking up blocks and carrying them around, to the advanced stages of creating complex structures that are a part of cooperative dramatic play, block building challenges children. As your children explore unit blocks, you will see them progress through these basic stages of block play.

Carrying—Children carry the blocks around the room, putting them into containers and taking them out, generally by themselves.

Stacking—Children stack the blocks in identical rows, either in small piles or laid flat, like roads. This is usually done alone, or sometimes alongside another child.

Bridging and Enclosing—Children make bridges and enclose spaces with the blocks, usually alone, but sometimes with another child or two. (Bridging and enclosing are two of the first ways children solve problems with blocks. Encourage these big steps in development.)

Patterning—Children build structures extending upward vertically with repeated patterns and symmetry, often done with others.

Representing—Children pretend and talk in small groups as constructions are built. They use accessories to play with a creation that is named after it is completed.

Dramatic Play—Children plan a complex construction cooperatively with other children, usually naming it before it is built. Using a variety of blocks and accessories, the children talk, pretend, and play.

Ways to Encourage Block Play Development

You will find that your children are at various stages of block play development. Post a list of the developmental stages of block play in the block area to help you observe where each child is now. Following are some suggestions for ways you can encourage the children to move on to the next stage of development.

- Give your children words that tell them what they are doing and that show you value their activity. "I see that you've put two square blocks and two cylinders into the bucket. You made them fit! Now what will you do?" (*Carrying* to *Stacking*)

- Praise all efforts, describing what they have done. "What a long road you've made. You used many long and short rectangles and you really worked hard. You should be very proud! Where does your road go?" (*Stacking* to *Bridging and Enclosing*)

- "You say your road goes to your grandma's house. Would you like me to get you more blocks so you can make her house?" (*Stacking* to *Bridging and Enclosing* or *Patterning*)

- "Wow! Look at all the bridges you made right next to each other. I see four bridges in a row. Is there a way you could make more bridges on top of these? Let's try it." (*Bridging and Enclosing* to *Patterning*)

- "You made a house. Do you need some dollhouse furniture and some little people? A car?" (*Patterning* to *Representing*)

- Ask questions that challenge children to think, guess, and solve problems, such as: "Is this road as long as you are? How do you think you could find out? What could you do to make your road longer? How many more blocks do you think you need?" or "You made a corral to keep your horses enclosed inside this space, but what if your horses want to go to the barn? How could you make a gate?" (*Representing* to *Dramatic Play*)

Storing Unit Blocks

Providing storage shelves protects your unit block investment and, most importantly, invites more constructive block play. If the blocks are just dumped into a bin or a box, your children will not be able to find the blocks they need, and their play will most likely be disorderly and infrequent. (Bin or box storage can also damage the blocks.) Store unit blocks in an inviting, orderly way on low, open shelves so the children can see each type of block. Arrange the blocks with the largest, heaviest blocks on the bottom shelves. Where each type of block goes on the shelf, draw an outline of it. Store block accessories in bins on top of the block shelves, labeling the bins with pictures for easy identification.

Cleanup Tips

Cleaning up can be challenging, no matter what needs to be put away. However, blocks are especially discouraging for young children because when they are all spread out it looks like cleaning them up is an *enormous* job. Try these tips to help block cleanup go a little smoother.

- About five minutes before cleanup time, let the children know that it will soon be time to clean up.

- When it is time for cleanup, use a visual or auditory signal (flashing a light, ringing a bell, etc.) that lets the children know it is time to clean up. Expect each child to help in some way. Let them know what activity will follow cleanup to give them a purpose.

- Show your children how to make piles of the same types of blocks. Then have them carry the blocks and place them on the shelves. Point out how piling the blocks up ahead of time makes the job of putting them on the shelves quick and easy.

- Matching blocks to places on the shelves is like a game. Encourage this fun activity with children who are hesitant to build; it will introduce them to the blocks in a comfortable way.

Supervising Block Play

Your physical presence in the block area and your attentive, interested observation of your children's play is the best possible technique for guiding block play and preventing problems. But your children will still need a few rules to guide them, and children follow rules best when they help develop them. Lead a guided discussion during group time to help your children make block safety rules like the following.

- Keep block structures smaller than yourself.

- Walk around the blocks, not on them.

- Never throw blocks.

- Build block structures with lots of room around them for walking.

- Only the builders can knock down their block constructions.

- Blocks are used for building, not for weapons.

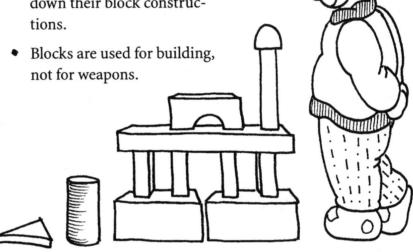

Taking Turns

Having enough blocks and accessories is the best way to reduce problems with sharing. You can also consider limiting the number of children who can play in the block area at one time by posting a sign with a drawing that shows the number of children allowed. Teach your children to use positive language to encourage taking turns, such as: "I've been waiting a long time; can I have a turn now?" or "May I use this piece now to make my bridge?"

Unit Blocks and Divergent Thinking

Divergent thinkers are people who know there are many answers to a question and many ways to solve a problem. Using open-ended materials, such as unit blocks, will get your children thinking in this way. Dealing with the challenges of block building makes the "wheels turn" in their heads, giving them infinite possibilities for improvising or creating. When something does not balance or look right to them, they will try constructing it in a new and different way. By exploring and discovering what works and what does not work while they play with unit blocks, your children are doing hands-on problem solving and becoming divergent thinkers.

Unit Blocks and Perceptual Skills

Perceptual skills lay the foundation for reading, writing, math, and science. These skills include eye-hand coordination, matching, sorting, estimating space, observing, and comparing. Your children practice eye-hand coordination and matching as they sort and pile up different shapes and sizes of blocks and use the blocks to build. They will begin to notice differences between blocks as they compare, sort, and match them. As the children build, they will develop and practice their spatial skills, making mental and visual estimates of space and deciding which blocks they need next to continue building their structures.

Unit Blocks and Math Skills

When your children build with unit blocks they are experimenting with the basics of mathematics. Help them see and compare the patterns and relationships in the blocks and the structures they have made. Try the following tips for fostering your children's beginning math skills as they build.

- Have the children compare the sizes and shapes of individual blocks and structures. Encourage them to sort and match the blocks in many ways.

- Use size words, such as *tall*, *high*, *short*, *wide*, *narrow*, *long*, and *thin*, as you discuss the children's structures with them.

- Talk about spatial relationships, such as *over*, *under*, *on top of*, *before*, *behind*, *above*, and *below*, as the children are building.

- Let your children practice the concept of reversibility by helping them remember how they built a particular structure.

- Have the children count the blocks or order them by size. Talk about size and quantity using words such as *big*, *small*, *many*, *few*, *more*, *less*, *how many*, *first*, *next*, and *last*.

Unit Blocks and Science

The basis of scientific thinking is to observe, hypothesize or wonder what might happen if you did a particular thing, try out your hypothesis, discover what happens, and share with others what you learned. Help your children talk about their experimenting and discoveries as they use the blocks. Let them explore and discuss the properties of the blocks they use. Give the children yarn, string, or a measuring tape to measure blocks and their constructions. Help them discover the principles of balance and notice what kind of structures have the best balance.

Unit Blocks and Music

There are many ways to combine music and your children's unit block play. Here are a few.

- Use unit blocks to make rhythm instruments. Give each child two short rectangles or two squares to rub together. Or let the children use pairs of cylinders as rhythm sticks, tapping them together gently.

- Play soft, peaceful instrumental music as the children build with the blocks. Observe how it affects their building. Try other kinds of music as well.

- Introduce your children to the concept of patterns in music and block building. Clap out a rhythmic beat with your hands and ask the children to clap with you. Build a simple structure using a pattern, such as a tower built with 1 rectangle, 2 squares, 1 rectangle, 2 squares. Have the children identify the pattern. Encourage the children to think of other patterns in music or their block building.

- Use blocks to represent clapping rhythms. For example, a rectangle block could mean slow clapping and a circle block could mean fast clapping. Put out several rectangle and circle blocks. As you point to each block, have your children clap the appropriate way.

Unit Blocks and Cooperation

Unit blocks inspire cooperation among your children more than many other materials in your classroom. As the children build, they discover that more interesting, complex structures can be built when several of them work together and share ideas. They also find that pretending and dramatic dialogue are more fun when you do them with friends. While disagreements will still occur, you can help your children the most by using the following tips.

- Point out that when they work together, the job (carrying, building, cleaning up) is easier and faster.

- Praise the children every time they cooperate as a group. Make it a point to describe the helping behaviors you see.

- Teach the children to say what they want or need in words, using *please* and *thank you.*

- Reinforce the idea that the blocks belong to everyone and that the children need to share them, take turns, and sometimes wait for what they want.

Making Your Own Accessories

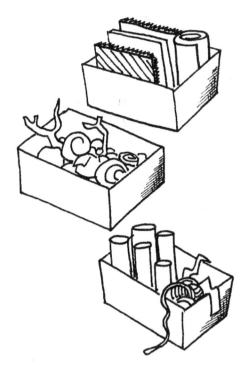

In addition to readymade accessories, there are many you and your children can find or make. Sort and store the following items in small plastic boxes for frequent use with the unit blocks.

- Scraps of carpet, fake fur, tiles, and linoleum samples

- Stones, rocks, shells, and small sticks or twigs

- Small pieces of plywood or pegboard for roofs and bridges

- Containers such as jewelry boxes and empty film canisters

- Furniture made from small scraps of wood, wooden or plastic spools, and glue

- Familiar store signs and traffic signs made from heavy paper glued to craft sticks and mounted on modeling dough bases

- Trees and flowers made like the signs above

- Silk flowers and colorful plastic grass for hay and straw

- Cardboard tubes for tunnels

- String, yarn, ribbon, lengths of fine chain, and pieces of small rubber tubing

Using Accessories With Unit Blocks

Adding accessories increases the range of dramatic play and language your children use as they play with unit blocks. As the children become interested in having realistic details for acting out their dramas, basic accessories, such as toy people, cars, trucks, boats, airplanes, trains, farm animals, and zoo animals, become important to their play. To make it easy for the children to see what accessories are available, sort them by type, and store them in see-through bins near the blocks.

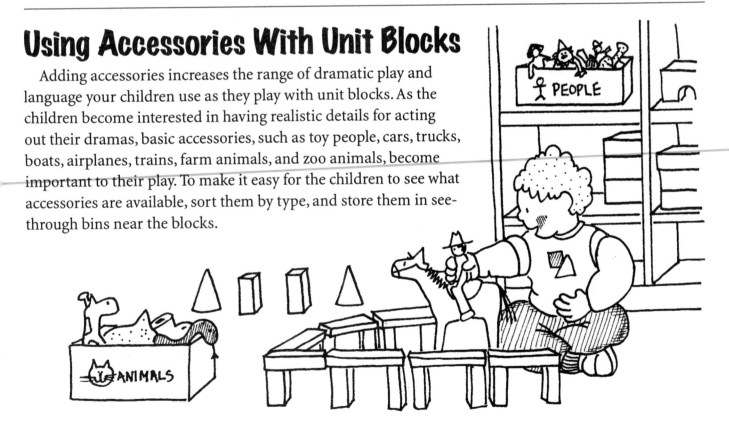

Unit Block Learning Games

Use unit blocks to make these quick and easy learning games for your children.

Find the Shape—Hide several different unit block shapes around the room. Show your children a block that is just like one of the blocks you hid. Ask them to find the matching-shaped block. Make the game more challenging by adding more shapes to remember and find.

Fill a Letter—Outline the letter *L* on the floor with masking tape. Ask your children to guess how many blocks it will take to fill up the letter. Have them try it and find out.

Make a Person—Draw a face on a paper plate. Place the plate on the floor. Have your children use basic square and rectangle blocks to make the torso and other body parts to go with the face.

Make a Pattern—Use the unit blocks to make a simple pattern on the floor. For example, you could make a pattern of square-triangle-square-triangle or short cylinder-long cylinder-short cylinder-long cylinder. Invite your children to repeat or continue the pattern. Increase the complexity of the patterns as the children's skills increase.

Unit Blocks and Motor Skills

To help your children develop and practice their eye-hand coordination and other small motor skills, plan activities such as the following.

Balancing—Have the children arrange a row of blocks, balanced on top of long rectangle blocks.

Block Match—Place a large piece of butcher paper on the floor. Let your children use pencils to carefully trace around many different types of blocks. Mix up the blocks and then have the children match the blocks to their outlines.

Build This—Build a simple block structure with five or six blocks. Ask the children to make a structure that looks just like it. As their skills increase, build the structure, have the children study it, then collapse it before they begin building an identical structure.

Jumping—Place a short cylinder on top of a square. Have the children act out the nursery rhyme "Jack Be Nimble" by jumping over the block "candle."

Unit Blocks and Dramatic Play

Dramatic play comes naturally during block building. When your children build a unit block creation and pretend with it, they are doing dramatic play. With the hands-on materials of blocks and accessories, the children can wonder, discover, and fantasize as they develop and act out stories. Through blocks, the children do things that would otherwise be impossible: create and fly spaceships, build cities and castles, or run a farm or a zoo. Following are some ideas you can use to spark your children's dramatic play in the block area.

- Encourage your children to make a store and sell the blocks. They can sell the blocks "as is" or pretend that the blocks are food, books, toys, or anything else they can imagine.

- Let the children take the blocks out of the block area and incorporate them into their dramatic play at other centers. For example, if the kitchen area needs more food, unit blocks can become baby bottles, toast, cakes, or whatever is needed. If a pretend campfire needs kindling and wood, cylinders and short rectangles work well.

- Invite your children to use the unit blocks to act out nursery rhymes. For example, rectangle blocks can be made into a brick wall for Humpty Dumpty to fall off of, or two square blocks can be curds and whey for Miss Muffet. Let the children think of other favorite rhymes to act out.

- Blocks can become trains or trucks, car ferries, docks, suspension bridges, lighthouses, mountains, high-rise apartments, trailer parks, or pueblos. Let the children's interests and cultures influence their play.

Successful Themes and Props for Unit Block Play

Because unit blocks are an open-ended material, they can be used with many classroom themes. For example, if the theme is community helpers, you could add the appropriate accessories (toy people, small signs, emergency vehicles, etc.) to encourage block play about community helpers. However, be sure to allow the children to use the blocks in any appropriate way. Following are some ideas for themes that work especially well with unit blocks.

Homes—Encourage your children to talk about and describe where they live. Discuss the many different kinds of homes people live in. Provide toy people, pets, furniture, cars, and trees. Let them use the unit blocks to make a variety of homes, such as houses, trailers, high-rise apartments, farms, and houseboats.

Transportation—Hang up pictures about transportation where your children can see them while building. Provide toy cars, trucks, boats, planes, trains, and other vehicles. Include toy people and cargo for transporting, such as wood scraps, pebbles, buttons, toy animals, and nuts and bolts. Invite your children to make roads, gas stations, rest stops, stores, train tracks, docks, and more.

Traffic Safety—Expand the setup described in Transportation at left, by adding many of the kinds of traffic signs your children see. (See Making Your Own Accessories on page 17, if you wish.) Talk about safety rules with people and vehicles, and let the children practice these rules with the blocks and toy cars.

The Farm—Hang up farm pictures in the block area. Provide toy people and farm animals. Have your children make the buildings and fences they want on their farm. Talk about what people and animals do on a farm.

The Zoo—Try this unit before or after a trip to the zoo. Put up pictures of zoo animals. Provide your children with toy animals and people. Discuss what a zoo looks like. Help the children think of good areas for zoo animals to live. Encourage them to build a special area for each kind of animal.

Building Vocabulary With Unit Blocks

There are many opportunities for expanding your children's vocabulary as they play in the block area. Following are a few ideas to get you started.

- Every day, use some of the math and science words discussed on page 15. Your children will quickly learn to use them correctly. Also learn and model the correct names of the blocks: *arch, half arch, half circle, cylinder, triangle, ramp, pillar, switch, square, rectangle.*

- Sit on the floor with a pencil and a tablet. Ask the children to tell you about what they are doing with the blocks. Write down all of the action words (*stack, pass, carry, pile, match, bridge, connect, make, build, cooperate,* etc.). Post their list of words in the block area.

- Encourage the children to name their unit block structures. Make a sign for each child or group of children, with the name of the structure on it. Let them put the sign on or by their structures.

Block Building Book

Sometimes your children work so hard together on a particular structure or become so engrossed in their play that they don't want to dismantle what they have built. When this happens, you may want to put a "Please save" sign on the structure. Explain the children's plans to the other children and take precautions to keep the structure standing. That day or the next, take photos of the builders' creation and let them tell you all about it. Write down what they say about who made it, how they did it, and what they pretended after it was built. Put the photo and their story on a large sheet of construction paper and cover it with clear self-stick paper. Collect these stories and bind them together to make a "Big Book About Our Blocks." Sometimes the children will use this book as a reference to rebuild a structure that they really liked.

Retelling Stories With Unit Blocks

Unit block play can be enhanced when used with storytelling. Select a story to read to your children. Choose one that they know by heart, such as a classic folk tale or story that you read to them often. Be sure that there are just a few characters in the story to make it easier to follow along. Also think about the number of props that will be required, because the fewer that are needed, the better. Sit in the block area and read or tell the story to your children. Encourage them to begin using the blocks to act out the story. If necessary, ask questions to facilitate the building: "Which block will be Little Red Riding Hood? Where should Grandma's house be? Where is the forest?"

Favorite Stories to Act Out

Here are several stories that work well for acting out with unit blocks.

"Goldilocks and the Three Bears"—Have your children use big, medium, and small blocks as needed. If they are skilled builders, encourage them to build the bears' house before beginning the story.

"The Three Little Pigs"—Provide accessories so that the straw house can have plastic-grass "straw" on its roof and the twig house can have a real twig roof. Give the children a toy wolf and three toy pigs, or help them select appropriate blocks to represent the characters.

The Little House—This book by Virginia Burton is a children's classic. Invite your children to build the little house and all of the city buildings that gradually surround her. Let them think of a way to move her to the country. Provide accessories as needed, such as plastic grass, toy animals, and tiny trees and silk flowers.

When I Build

Sung to: "Twinkle, Twinkle, Little Star"

When I build with blocks today,

I will build things just this way.

I will build them up and down

To make a rocket or a town.

I will build things just like so.

Building blocks are fun, I know.

Gayle Bittinger

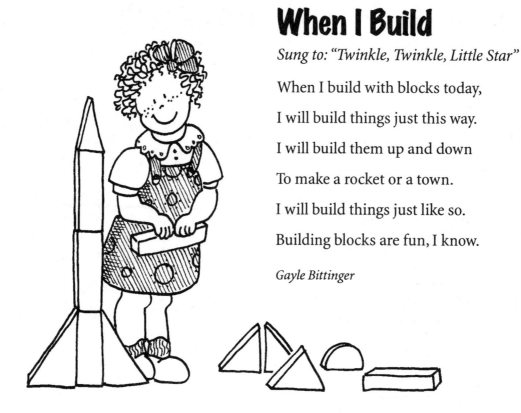

I'm a Builder

Sung to: "Frère Jacques"

I'm a builder, I'm a builder.

Yes, I am. Yes, I am.

I can build a fort,

I can build a fort

With my hands, with my hands.

Substitute the names of other structures
your children are building for *fort*.

Jean Warren

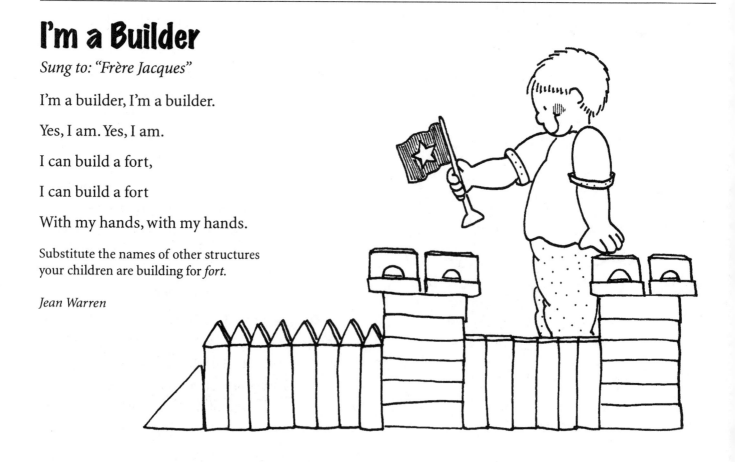

Cleaning Up

Sung to: "Frère Jacques"

Cleaning up, cleaning up

All the blocks, all the blocks.

First we sort and pile them,

First we sort and pile them,

One by one, one by one.

Cleaning up, cleaning up

All the blocks, all the blocks.

Next we all arrange them,

Next we all arrange them

On the shelf, on the shelf.

Cleaning up, cleaning up

All the blocks, all the blocks.

Cleaning up together,

Cleaning up together

Makes it fast, makes it fast.

Gayle Bittinger

Building a City

Sung to: "Jingle Bells"

Build a street, build a park,

Build a home for me.

It's so fun to plan and build

A great big city.

Build a school, build a bridge,

Build a grocery store.

With each place you build with blocks

Your city grows some more.

Gayle Bittinger

Hollow Blocks

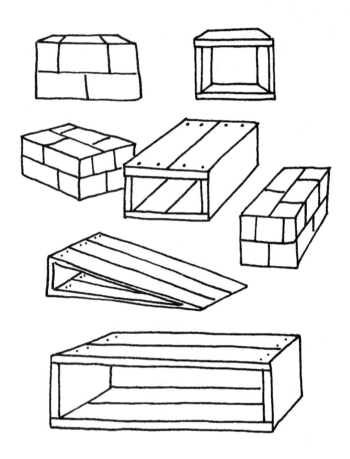

What Are Hollow Blocks?

Hollow blocks are much bigger than unit blocks and are designed to encourage your children to build actual sets for their dramatic play. When the children create ships, docks, vehicles, and buildings with hollow blocks, they become the actors in their dramas. There are two types of hollow blocks. Cardboard hollow blocks are decorated to look like bricks. They come in several colors and are fairly inexpensive. These blocks will wear out and must be replaced on a regular basis. Maple or hardwood hollow blocks are expensive, but they will last for many years without showing wear. They are sturdier than cardboard blocks and are built precisely like unit blocks. In addition to the basic rectangle, hardwood hollow blocks also come in squares, boards, and triangle ramps.

Why Use Hollow Blocks?

In addition to providing many of the benefits that other block play encourages, hollow blocks add another dimension to your children's block play. Following are a few reasons for including them in your classroom.

- Hollow blocks are an open-ended material and your children will successfully find many ways to use them.

- Hollow block play lets the children investigate how people work and play together.

- As the children build with hollow blocks they act out roles, helping them develop and practice their vocabulary and language skills.

- The children learn to share ideas and respect the ideas of others.

- Hollow blocks are easy to integrate with many themes.

- Hollow block play encourages your children to practice many motor skills.

- Hollow blocks teach the children real construction techniques.

- The children feel pride and accomplishment building with big blocks.

When to Use Hollow Blocks

Have hollow blocks available during free choice time. However, for hollow block play to remain safe and positive, it is best to encourage your children to build with the big blocks only when they have a particular purpose or plan in mind.

Where to Use Hollow Blocks

Hollow block play is often active and dramatic and needs floor space of its own. Locate the hollow block play area near the unit block area, because advanced block builders often want to use the two kinds of blocks together. Hollow blocks also go well with additional large props such as climbers or small riding toys. You will need additional floor space if you want to let your children incorporate these large props into their play.

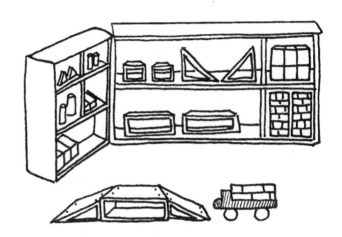

How Many Do You Need?

Check school supply stores and catalogs to compare prices, quality, and varieties of hollow blocks. When purchasing hardwood hollow blocks, most groups will need at least 40 pieces, comprised of rectangles, squares, ramps, and boards. (This is sometimes referred to as a "half school set.") Teach the children to stack and store hollow blocks neatly against one wall of the block area.

Supervising Hollow Block Play

The key to supervising hollow block play is preventing problems. Having a teacher available to supervise the block area throughout free choice time is invaluable for constructive play. Following are a few tips for watching over the hollow block area.

Preventing Problems—Prevent problems by offering suggestions, making positive comments, and gathering props.

Resolving Conflicts—When there is a conflict, help facilitate problem-solving among the children using these steps:

- Have each child explain what he or she thinks the problem is.

- Ask each child what solution he or she would suggest.

- Have the children choose one of the solutions to try. Move on to additional solutions, if necessary.

- Praise the children for their problem-solving efforts.

Making Rules—Help your children make rules for hollow block play, such as:

- Take apart hollow block structures slowly and safely, handing down top blocks first.

- Any change to the structure must be agreed upon by all of the builders.

- Big blocks cannot be used to cage monsters.

Waiting for a Turn—If you limit the number of children that can play with the hollow blocks at one time, decorate a special "waiting chair" and place it next to the hollow block play area. Remind the active builders that others need to have their turn as well.

Hollow Blocks Across the Curriculum

Hollow blocks can be used to teach a variety of skills and concepts to your children. Here are a few ideas.

Motor Development—Use hollow blocks to provide opportunities for the children to lift, carry, walk, climb, and stretch. Combine hollow blocks with steps, carpet squares, hoops, or mats to create an obstacle course to allow your children to practice motor skills.

Math—Give your children a ruler or a measuring tape to measure their structures. Encourage them to count blocks as they build.

Dramatic Play—Let your children act out many different roles as they play with and in the structures they build. Help them think and talk about what their different roles are.

Science—Point out the ways your children are learning about balance and support. Help them notice when blocks are balanced and when they are not. Have them carefully observe structures that are sturdy and have adequate support and those that do not.

Self-Esteem—Help your children feel proud of the hollow block structures they build. Talk about the many skills they used to build their structures.

Respect—Teach your children respect as they work together to build their structures. Help them share ideas, negotiate, compromise, and solve problems to reach a common goal.

Hollow Blocks and Language

As your children talk about what they are doing in the hollow block area, they begin to find and use words that describe their movements. Encourage them to use these words throughout the day. Display pictures that will give them new ideas and vocabulary for their dramatic play with the blocks. Ask the children to tell you about their structures by asking questions such as: "Can you tell me about this? What kind of blocks did you use? How did you make this part? What is the best part? What will you do here?"

Retelling Stories

Hollow blocks are perfect for making "sets" for acting out familiar stories and rhymes. Here are a few ideas to get you and your children started.

- Make a bridge for the goats and troll in the story "The Three Billy Goats Gruff."

- Create a train engine and cars for acting out *The Little Engine That Could.*

- Construct a haystack for Little Boy Blue and act out the nursery rhyme.

- Make the buildings and vehicles in the wordless book *Changes, Changes* by Pat Hutchins, and act out the story.

Tips on Integrating Themes

The open-ended nature of hollow blocks makes the hollow block area a perfect place for your children to explore any theme or topic they are learning about. Here are some tips for integrating themes into hollow block play.

- Collect the needed props and accessories to complement your theme. (Invite parents to help gather props and other materials for the theme.) Make the props accessible, but allow the children to play and build with the hollow blocks as they wish.

- Be flexible. If your theme on transportation is over, but the children are still making vehicles with hollow blocks for dramatic play, let them do it. If they build a hospital and you are not "doing" community helpers yet, you should still encourage their work.

- Be open and spontaneous. Let your children think of what they want to build. If you take a trip to an apple orchard during your apple theme, the children may be interested in creating rows of apple trees with the hollow blocks, or they may want to build a replica of the wagon that took them for a ride.

Hollow Blocks and Dramatic Play

Hollow blocks invite dramatic play. Watch as the children build with one idea and adapt and change it as they play. It is this process, not a particular end product, that is important. Here are a few more things to keep in mind as you and your children explore dramatic play with hollow blocks.

- Develop prop boxes for particular play sets (see pages 35–45). Collect the appropriate props and put them in sturdy boxes with lids. (Cardboard office storage boxes work well for this.)

- Give the children plenty of time to enjoy the fun of building a "set" with the blocks. If necessary, show them how to use the hollow blocks to make walls, furniture, and other props they might need.

- Guide the children in acting out the various roles that a particular set suggests. This gives your children a way to release energy and express all kinds of feelings.

- Help the children practice and learn ways of coping with a new or a possibly uncomfortable experience (riding a school bus, going to the doctor, moving to a new home) by building an appropriate set and acting out what happens.

- Observe each child as he or she plays to gain insight into his or her skills, personality, self-image, strengths, weaknesses, needs, and fears.

- Guide the children, if needed, but concentrate on observing. Join in the play, if invited.

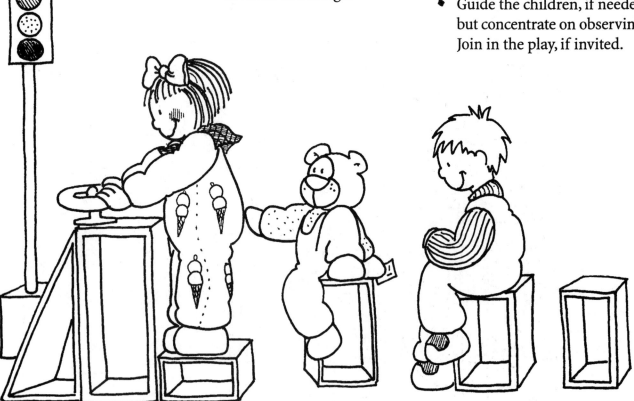

Toy Store

Let your children use the hollow blocks to make a toy store with the appropriate display shelves and counter. Ask them to decide on a name for their store.

- Small toys suitable for displaying on block shelves

- Toy grocery cart or basket

- Toy cash register and play money

- Apron for salesperson

- Telephone, notepad, and pen

- Large sheets of paper and crayons for making signs

- Canvas bags or cardboard boxes for packaging up purchases

Welcome to Our Store

Sung to: "Twinkle, Twinkle, Little Star"

Welcome, welcome to our store,

We have lots of toys galore.

You will find toys all around,

We have the best toys in town.

Come and look at all our toys,

Fun for girls and fun for boys.

Gayle Bittinger

Gas Station

Encourage your children to use the hollow blocks to create a gas station. If needed, ask them questions to get them started, such as: "Where will cars pull up? Where will the drivers pay? Is there a car wash at your gas station?"

- Gas pump made from a hose (old section of garden hose or a leftover spray nozzle and hose from a sink) taped to a pump (a chair, a large box, or other suitable base)

- Toy telephone and an old walkie-talkie set for dispatching a tow truck

- Keys of all kinds, with cup hooks on a board to hang them on

- Small, clean oil cans and a red plastic jug labeled "gas"

- Sponges, rags, and small buckets to "wash" vehicles

- Pliers, wrenches, and other tools

- Nuts, bolts, and clamps

- Tire pump and bicycle inner tubes

- Road maps, flashlights, play money, receipt book, and price signs

I Take Care of Your Car

Sung to: " Frère Jacques"

Pumping gas, pumping gas

With my hose, with my hose.

I take care of your car,

So you can travel far.

Pump, pump, pump,

Pump, pump, pump.

Cleaning windows, cleaning windows

With a towel, with a towel.

I take care of your car,

So you can travel far.

Wipe, wipe, wipe,

Wipe, wipe, wipe.

Filling tires, filling tires

With some air, with some air.

I take care of your car,

So you can travel far.

Ssss, ssss, ssss,

Ssss, ssss, ssss.

Jean Warren

Space Shuttle

Let your children's imaginations soar as they design and build their very own space shuttle out of hollow blocks. Talk about what they might be seeing as they fly along in their shuttle.

- Space suits (tunics or vests) sewn from gray or silver fabric or found at a secondhand store

- Old "moon boots" for space boots

- Space helmets made from 5-gallon cardboard ice cream tubs (available from ice cream stores) with rectangles cut out to see through

- Old flashlights, binoculars, cameras, watches, compasses, small coolers, small boxes for collecting "moon rocks," and rocks

- Odds and ends of tubes and hoses

- Space "food"

- Cardboard "computer," electronic displays, and a steering wheel

- First-aid kit, name tags, security badges, an old radio, and walkie-talkies

- Music to play during space shuttle play, such as the song "Space Travel" from the recording *On the Move* by Greg and Steve

Our Station in the Sky

Sung to: "If You're Happy and You Know It"

Oh, we're living in our station in the sky,

Oh, we're living in our station in the sky.

We sleep here and we eat,

And it really is a treat.

Oh, we're living in our station in the sky.

Oh, we're living in our station in the sky,

Oh, we're living in our station in the sky.

We take a walk in space,

Yes, we really love this place,

Oh, we're living in our station in the sky.

Jean Warren

Camping

Help your children create a camping area with hollow blocks. Talk about what a campsite might have: a table, a fire pit, a faucet for getting water, and so on.

- Real or improvised sleeping bags
- Fabric or sheet to use to make a tent
- Canteens, water jug, plastic dishes, dishtub, and towels
- Small cooler and pretend food such as empty cans and boxes
- Paper bag or wastebasket for collecting "trash"
- Clothesline and spring-type clothespins
- Flashlights
- Small backpacks
- First-aid kit
- Pair of old binoculars, camera, radio, and maps
- "Kindling" and other blocks for a campfire and red cellophane for a "fire"

A-Camping We Will Go

Sung to: "The Farmer in the Dell"

A-camping we will go,

A-camping we will go,

Heigh-ho the derry-oh,

A-camping we will go.

We'll sleep under the stars,

We'll sleep under the stars.

Heigh-ho the derry-oh,

We'll sleep under the stars.

We'll take a nature hike,

We'll take a nature hike.

Heigh-ho the derry-oh,

We'll take a nature hike.

We'll roast some marshmallows,

We'll roast some marshmallows.

Heigh-ho the derry-oh,

We'll roast some marshmallows.

Continue with additional verses about other camping activities.

Jean Warren

Office

Let your children design their office space with room for desks, chairs, shelves, computers, phones, and other office essentials.

- Old typewriter or computer keyboard
- Paper, carbon paper, pens and pencils, pencil holder
- Envelopes, junk mail, old cards, and trading stamps
- Hole punch and stapler
- Rubber stamps and ink pads
- Several telephones (real, nonworking phones work well)
- Briefcases, totebags, and lunch sacks
- Glasses with the lenses removed
- Clock

At My Office

Sung to: "Did You Ever See a Lassie?"

I work hard at my office,

My office, my office.

I work hard at my office.

I work hard all day,

Writing and talking

And typing and thinking.

I work hard at my office,

I work hard all day.

I work hard at my office,

My office, my office.

I work hard at my office.

I work hard all day,

Sorting and stapling

And stamping and reading.

I work hard at my office,

I work hard all day.

Jean Warren

Restaurant

Show your children how to use the hollow blocks to build a restaurant with an entrance or waiting area, tables to eat at, and a kitchen area.

- Tablecloths, centerpieces (consider plastic or silk plants and flowers), and votive candles with the wicks cut off

- Cloth napkins, empty salt and pepper shakers, sugar bowl, and pitcher

- Real restaurant menus (local restaurants may be willing to donate old ones) and pictures of restaurant foods or meals

- Aprons, order pads, and pencils

- Chef's hat, cooking utensils, and pretend foods

- Play telephone for taking reservations and orders "to go"

- Signs for hours, prices, open, and closed

- Play money and cash register or till

At Our Restaurant

Sung to: "When Johnny Comes Marching Home"

Please come and eat at our restaurant today, today.

We hope you'll come to eat with us and stay, and stay.

We'll take your order, we'll bring you food,

We know that you'll think it's really good.

Oh, please come eat at our restaurant today.

Jean Warren

Fire Station

Fire stations are particularly interesting when combined with a climber and slide. Hollow blocks are also fun to use outdoors to add enjoyment, interest, and variety. Encourage your children to build a fire station and hollow block structures that catch on "fire."

- Firefighting clothes such as big overcoats, helmets, and boots
- Varied lengths of hoses and ropes (old vacuum cleaner hoses are great); be sure to remove any sharp or metal ends
- Firefighter badges and megaphone (a large funnel works well) for the fire chief
- Bell for an alarm, toy telephones, and old walkie-talkies
- Fire engine made of blocks or a fire engine riding toy

Down by the Station

Sung to: "Down by the Station"

Down by the station

Early in the morning,

See the great big firetrucks

Standing in a row.

See the busy firefighters

Hanging up the hoses.

Huff-huff, huff-huff,

Watch them go.

Down by the station

Early in the morning,

See the great big firetrucks

Standing in a row.

See the busy firefighters

Washing all the engines,

Scrub-scrub, scrub-scrub,

Watch them go.

Down by the station

Early in the morning,

See the great big firetrucks

Standing in a row.

See the busy firefighters

Starting up the engines,

Clang-clang, clang-clang,

Watch them go.

Jean Warren

Hospital

Playing hospital with hollow blocks helps young children reduce their fears and feel more comfortable in a medical setting. Let them use the blocks to make spaces for a waiting room and beds for "patients." For variety, have the children create a veterinarian's office another day.

- Appropriate signs, pictures, and books

- Small blankets and pillow

- Dolls and stuffed animals for patients

- Wide cardboard tubes cut into small sections for arm and wrist casts

- X-rays (ask your doctor or hospital for old ones)

- Uniforms made of old green or white shirts with the sleeves cut short and worn backwards, or used uniforms found at a thrift store and cut down to size

- Doctor's bags (old black purses work well)

- Medical supplies such as a small flashlight, hair tape or regular bandages, old elastic bandages, stethoscope, and latex gloves (inexpensively purchased at a medical supply store if not donated)

I Am a Doctor

Sung to: "My Bonnie Lies Over the Ocean"

I'm happy that I am a doctor,

'Cause I help to make people well.

I'm happy that I am a doctor;

When I help, it makes me feel swell.

I'm a doctor,

And I help people feel

Well, well, well.

I'm a doctor,

I feel happy, can't you tell?

Jean Warren

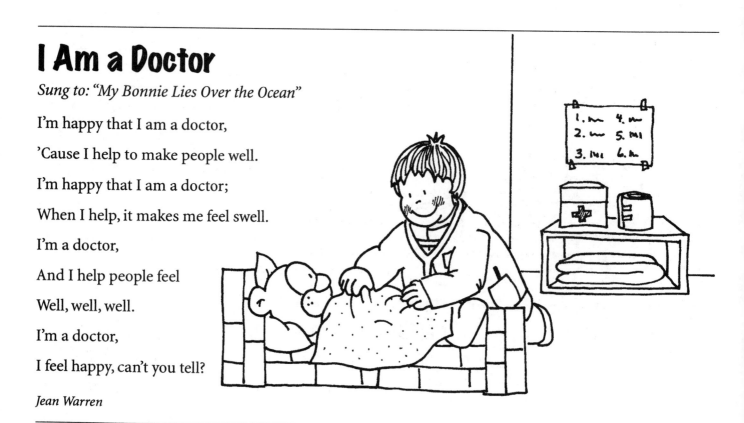

Boat

The type of boat play your children engage in is influenced by their experiences and local geography or culture. Be sure to include boating props specific to the area you live in. Let your children decide what kind of boat (ferryboat, rowboat, fishing boat, canoe, cruise ship, sailboat, etc.) they would like to build with the hollow blocks. Have pictures on hand to inspire them, if you wish. Suggest building a pier, a wharf, or a dock as well.

- Various lengths of rope
- Life jackets (talk about boat and water safety)
- Styrofoam wreath (available at craft stores) with a short length of rope attached for use as a "life-saving" ring
- Radio, binoculars, camera, and walkie-talkies
- Snorkels, masks, and fins
- Sunglasses, empty bottles of sunscreen, and hats or visors
- Fishing poles made of dowels with short lengths of string attached

A-Sailing We Will Go

Sung to: "The Farmer in the Dell"

A-sailing we will go,

A-sailing we will go.

Heigh-ho the derry-oh,

A-sailing we will go.

We built a great big boat,

We built a great big boat.

Heigh-ho the derry-oh,

We built a great big boat.

Let's all climb aboard,

Let's all climb aboard.

Heigh-ho the derry-oh,

Let's all climb aboard.

We'll put life jackets on,

We'll put life jackets on.

Heigh-ho the derry-oh,

We'll put life jackets on.

A-sailing we will go,

A-sailing we will go.

Heigh-ho the derry-oh,

A-sailing we will go.

Jean Warren

Train

When your children set out to create a train, encourage them to think about all the different train cars they would like to have. Will their train carry animals, people, toys, food, or something else? If the train will carry people, where will the people sit? Will their train have a caboose? If they wish, have them create a train station as well.

- Steering wheel mounted on a sturdy cardboard box

- Hats for the conductor and engineer

- Tools for repairing the train

- Tickets, play money, pads of paper, pencils, hole punches, and appropriate signs

- Small suitcases and backpacks for any travelers

- Cargo such as stuffed animals or pretend food

Climb Aboard

Sung to: "London Bridge"

Climb aboard and travel with us,

Travel with us, travel with us.

Climb aboard and travel with us

On our train.

We will go to cities and towns,

Cities and towns, cities and towns.

We will go to cities and towns

On our train.

We will carry toys and food,

Toys and food, toys and food.

We will carry toys and food

On our train.

Substitute the name of a particular place for *cities and towns*. Substitute the names of other goods the train could carry for *toys and food*.

Gayle Bittinger

Beach

There are a wide variety of beaches for your children to explore. Help them decide what their beach will look like and what sets they will need. Hollow blocks can be used for building a lifeguard tower, a fishing dock, a picnic table, a concession stand, and more.

- A string of floats to rope off a safe swimming area

- Life jackets and swimming inflatables

- Swim fins, snorkels, and masks

- Beach towels, beach shoes, sun hats, and sunglasses

- Picnic basket, pretend food and drinks, and a bag for collecting litter

- Buckets, shovels, and shells

The Beach Is Fun

Sung to: "Row, Row, Row Your Boat"

Watch us as we build

A place to swim and play.

The beach is fun for everyone,

We will stay all day.

Watch us as we build

A sandy place to play.

The beach is fun for everyone,

We will stay all day.

Gayle Bittinger

Table Blocks

What Are Table Blocks?

Table blocks, as the name suggests, are blocks that are small enough to be used at tables. Table blocks are often classified as manipulatives because children develop eye-hand coordination as they use them. Table blocks are made of wood or plastic and come in many colors, shapes, sizes, and types.

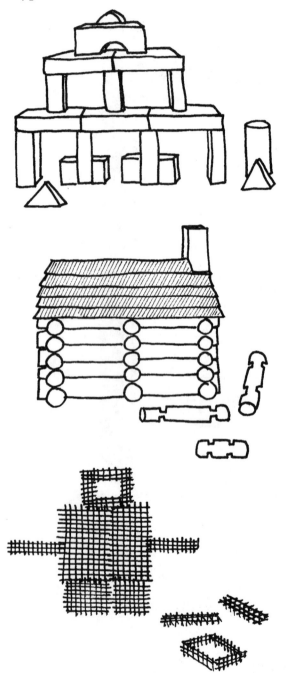

Why Use Table Blocks?

- Table blocks are an open-ended material and can be used in many ways by children of diverse ages, backgrounds, and abilities.

- Table blocks help your children practice concentration, increase attention, and develop creativity.

- Table blocks help your children practice eye-hand coordination and other small-motor skills.

- Table blocks provide opportunities for your children to practice math and problem-solving skills.

Where to Use Table Blocks

Most often, table blocks are used at tables in the small-muscle area, along with other manipulatives. However, many 3-year-olds and young 4-year-olds will want to use them on the floor. If this is the case with your children, try to have some floor space available in the small-muscle area for this kind of exploration.

When to Use Table Blocks

Have table blocks available at free choice time. Set out one kind of table block on a table before free choice time to entice your children to the area. Another time to use table blocks is as the children are coming to your program. Early arrivals can use the table blocks until the rest of the children are there.

Outfitting Your Room With Table Blocks

You can provide a variety of table block play experiences for your children with these kinds of table blocks.

Colored Shape Blocks—These blocks can be sorted by color or shape and used to build an endless variety of structures and towers decorated with half circles, triangles, and arches. Watch as your children practice concentration, balance, precision, and eye-hand coordination while they develop their unique creations. A set of 50 colored blocks works well for an average-size group.

Colored Wooden Cubes—Use these cubes for math activities such as sorting, patterning, and counting activities, as well as for building. They can also be used in conjunction with the colored shape blocks. A set of 100 cubes provides enough variety and challenge. Both these blocks and the colored shape blocks are sometimes borrowed to decorate unit block creations.

Wooden Snap Blocks—These blocks include cylinder and wheel shapes and have sturdy snaps attached to every side. Show your children how to easily connect them to make people, rolling vehicles, and unusual buildings. A set of 50 provides enough variety for beginners.

Plastic Bristle Blocks—Covered with safe, soft plastic bristles, these blocks can interlock at any point, making it easy for even the youngest child to make instant creations that stick together or pull apart. A set of 80 bristle blocks in various shapes makes it easy to play and share.

Wooden Log Blocks—These blocks are an all-time favorite with young children. Let your children explore how to use the interlocking logs, gables, chimneys, and roof pieces to make realistic log houses, cabins, forts, and villages for further creative play. A 150-piece set gives your creative builders a great start.

Plastic Interlocking Blocks—These durable bricks are a traditional favorite. For younger children, begin with the larger blocks (a set of 50 works fine). For older children (who will not put the blocks in their mouth), use the smaller plastic interlocking blocks. (A set of 400 small blocks with building bases allows room for creativity and cooperation.) Wheels and other accessories can be added to blocks of either size for making vehicles and other unique structures.

Supervising Table Block Play

Behavior management problems will be rare if you set a few simple guidelines and provide enough materials and space for table block play. Following are some suggestions.

- Purchase enough of each type of table block (see page 50) so that from one to five children can share and use them together.

- Allow enough table space for table block play. If possible, reserve one whole table for this kind of block play and another table for play with other types of manipulatives in your small-muscle area.

- Let the number of chairs at a table tell how many children can play at one time. If a child is waiting to play, write his or her name on a waiting list and then help the child find something else to do until a space opens up.

- Do not allow children to create guns or weapons from any of the table blocks. If this happens, state your rule about guns and weapons, then redirect the play with comments or questions, or by adding some new accessories.

- Use descriptive praise as a behavior management tool. Praise behavior you want children to repeat: "You helped Kayla build her fire engine. I noticed how you worked together to make that bridge. Thanks for putting those away so carefully."

Table Blocks and Themes

While the primary purpose of table blocks is to foster small-motor development, eye-hand coordination, and concentration skills, a variety of themes can be integrated into table block play. The easiest way to do this is to provide accessories that enhance the theme you are working on.

Space—Many kinds of accessories, especially for plastic interlocking blocks, can be purchased to encourage space play and design.

Community Helpers—Using toy people and vehicles lets your children explore various roles people have in a community. You may also be able to purchase or make toy signs to accompany your children's building.

Animals—Adding toy animals and people can inspire your children to build a zoo, a farm, or a veterinarian's office.

Playground—Because many of the table blocks interlock, they are ideal for creating playground equipment. Set out toy people for "playing" on the equipment your children design and build.

Homes and Families—Collect a variety of toy people (some table blocks have toy people designed especially for use with them). Set out pictures of families and homes, and let your children role-play as they build.

Using Table Blocks as Props

There are a variety of ways your children can use table blocks to expand their play in new and creative directions.

Table Blocks and Creativity—
Observe your children as they use various types of table blocks to make an assortment of props. Snap blocks or bristle blocks are turned into unique vehicles and fantasy creatures that are far more interesting than any purchased props. Plastic interlocking blocks with the accompanying wheels, flexible connectors, and other accessories make it possible for your children to create almost anything.

Table Blocks Together—Give
your children the opportunity to use various types of table blocks in combination. This allows the children limitless possibilities while building. For example, airplanes, helicopters, or spaceships built with snap blocks can be used in an airport or a space station built of wooden cubes. A dragon made of bristle blocks can be used with a plastic interlocking block castle.

Table Blocks and Other Manipulatives—Let your chil-
dren combine table blocks with the other manipulatives in the small-muscle area. (Be sure they sort and put away the blocks and manipulatives when they are finished.) Encourage the children's problem solving and creative thinking as they make props out of a nut and bolt set or some snap beads to use with a wooden log house. There are many combinations with which to experiment.

Table Blocks and Art

The very process of creating a structure, fantasy figure, or unusual vehicle from table blocks is art and the completed piece is a work of art. In addition to this creative process that happens naturally, you can help your children combine table blocks and art in other ways, such as the following.

Block Town—Spread a sheet of butcher paper over a table and tape it in place. Help your children create a map of a town with felt tip markers and crayons. Have them use the table blocks to make the necessary buildings, towers, bridges, and other structures to complete their town.

Decorations—Set out construction paper, scissors, crayons, and tape. Let the children design and cut out various decorations to add to their creations.

Rubbings—Have each of your children select a table block (bristle blocks or plastic interlocking blocks work especially well). Show them how to place a sheet of plain, white paper over the block and rub a crayon (with the wrapper removed) over the paper to create a design.

Table Blocks and Language

There are many ways to foster language development while your children are playing with table blocks. Here are a few ideas to try.

- When your children are creating things with table blocks, make a note of their interests and find books and pictures that reflect these. The books and pictures will help give the children new words to use while building, and will foster more ideas.

- Help your children make many kinds of small signs for their constructions.

- Keep a notepad and pencil in the small-muscle area. When your children tell stories about their creations, listen carefully and write down what they say. Later, print the words on big paper and let them see and hear the words of the story as they told it. Save space on the paper for their illustrations.

Table Blocks, Small-Motor Skills, and More

All table blocks help your children practice and improve eye-hand coordination, attention span, concentration, and other small-motor skills, as well as creative thinking and an understanding of cause and effect. Particular blocks also help the children with specific skills, such as the following.

Snap Blocks—Snap blocks improve your children's handling of small items; pressing, pulling, and connecting skills; and problem-solving skills.

Bristle Blocks—Bristle blocks give your children practice grasping, holding, pressing, pulling, connecting, and placing objects.

Wooden Log Blocks—Wooden log blocks help the children's skills in observing, concentrating, placement, balance, and solving problems.

Colored Shape Blocks—Colored shape blocks and colored wooden cubes help the children develop their creativity and problem-solving skills, as well as balance, placement, and concentration.

Plastic Interlocking Blocks—Plastic interlocking blocks help the children practice pressing, pulling, and connecting skills, and develop their creativity and problem-solving skills.

Table Blocks and Math

There are many ways to expand your children's math skills while they are playing with table blocks.

- Use math language whenever possible as the children use table blocks. For example, to discuss spatial relationships use descriptive words, such as *tall, short, wide, narrow, big,* and *small,* and positional words and phrases such as *on top of, under, next to,* and *on the corner.*

- Have the children count the blocks they are using. Ask: "How many blocks are in that tall tower?"

- Help the children compare the structures they make. Talk about more and less. Ask: "Which tower has more blocks, the tall one or the short one?"

Shape Games

Whenever your children play with colored shape blocks, they are learning about the properties of different shapes. Help the children take the next steps in understanding shapes by knowing and encouraging each of the following steps in the learning sequence.

Touch—Let your children enjoy the concrete experience of handling and sorting blocks in their own ways.

Match—Ask your children to find a block shaped like the one you are showing them or to pile up all the blocks shaped like it.

Find—Add the name of the shape to the matching experience. Ask your children to find a square just like this one or a circle like that one.

Label—When your children are ready for the last step, they will be able to find any shape of block you ask for without a visual cue.

Extension: You can also help your children learn colors following the same steps of touch, match, find, and label.

More Math Games

Colored shape blocks lend themselves well to individualized teaching, because a teacher and one or two children can sit together to play games that help each child practice specific skills. When a child has mastered the concept of shapes and colors, here are some additional games you can play.

* Add a counting aspect to a finding game. Ask the children to find three triangles, four squares, or five rectangles.

* Make a simple pattern with the blocks (blue square-red triangle-blue square-red triangle). Ask the children to find the block that comes next.

* Set out red, blue, and yellow blocks of square, triangle, and rectangle shapes. Ask the children to think of various ways to sort the blocks.

Here's a Shape

Sung to: "Frère Jacques"

Here's a triangle, here's a triangle

With three sides, with three sides.

If you count you'll see

Sides for 1-2-3.

Triangle, triangle.

Here's a square, here's a square

With four sides, with four sides.

You will find no more

Sides than 1-2-3-4.

Here's a square, here's a square.

Here's a rectangle, here's a rectangle

Short and long, short and long.

With two short and two long

Sides, you can't go wrong.

Rectangle, rectangle.

Gayle Bittinger

Hide and Seek

Select several colored shape blocks of the same color but different shapes. Hide the blocks in a dishpan or a box of sand. Ask your children to find a particular shape. Make the game more challenging by asking the children to find different numbers of two different shapes: "Find one red square and three red rectangles." As the children's skills increase, hide shapes of different colors. Ask them to find two different colors and shapes: "Find one red triangle and two yellow rectangles."

Can You Find?

Sung to: "Twinkle, Twinkle, Little Star"

Can you find this block for me?

Peek inside here carefully.

I hid some blocks for you to find,

Won't you stop and be so kind?

When you look perhaps you'll see

A blue triangle just for me.

Substitute the name of the block you would like your children to find for *blue triangle*.

Gayle Bittinger

Cube Pattern Fun

Use the colorful wooden cubes to make a simple pattern such as blue-yellow-blue-yellow or red-red-green-red-red-green. Show your children how to copy the pattern by placing matching cubes beside your row. After the children master copying a pattern, let them practice extending one. Start a pattern with the cubes, help the children name the pattern, and then let them continue it. Modify this game to fit various skill levels by using more or fewer cubes or simpler or more complex patterns.

Game Design

Place colored shape blocks flat on a table to make a design. Invite your children to make a copy of your design next to it. (Make the design simple or complicated, depending on the skill of your children.) Help the children create templates of their favorite designs so that they can play this game independently. Have them place white construction paper on the table, create a design on the paper, trace around each block, and use felt tip markers or crayons to fill in the color of each block. Let them re-create the design on the template or beside it.

Table Blocks and Science

Whenever your children use table blocks to make a structure or create something that rolls or "works," they are applying scientific principles. Here are some other ways your children can learn about science as they play.

- When your children handle table blocks, help them discover the properties of each block. What is its weight, shape, color, texture, and so on?

- Help the children make observations about the blocks as they build with them. What are the blocks made of? Are they shiny or dull? Are they smooth or bumpy?

- Encourage the children to think of ways to sort the blocks based on similar characteristics: size, texture, color, shape, shininess, etc.

- Hold out a handful of colorful wooden cubes. Ask the children to estimate how many you have. Count the blocks together and have the children compare their guesses with the actual number.

- Give the children a length of yarn. Ask them to build a tower as tall as the yarn.

Sorting Game

Put out a pile of various kinds of table blocks. Ask your children to sort them by color. Sing the following song. Repeat the song for each color of block the children are sorting. When they are finished, have them look at their work. Are all the blocks where they want them to be? Then mix up the blocks and have the children think of another way to sort them. Sing additional verses of the following song for this new way of sorting.

Sung to: "London Bridge"

When I look at all the blocks,

All the blocks, all the blocks,

When I look at all the blocks

I see red ones.

Gayle Bittinger

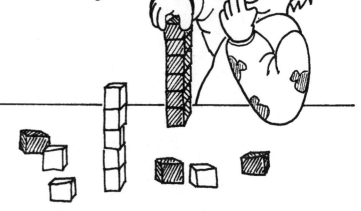

Tower Estimation

Build a tower with bristle blocks. Have your children look at the tower. Ask them to estimate how many plastic interlocking blocks they think it will take to make a tower the same size. Have them build the tower with the interlocking blocks and count them. How did their guesses compare to the real number? Make another bristle block tower of a different height. Ask the children to guess again how many interlocking plastic blocks it will take to build a tower the same size. Have them build the tower. Let them compare the number of blocks used with their guesses. Repeat with other sizes of towers and, if you wish, other kinds of table blocks.

Weighty Blocks

Set out a balance. Select two blocks that are the same size but different weights. Show the blocks to your children. Ask them to guess which one weighs more. Put a block in each of the balance pans. Which block is heavier? Add more of the lighter-weight blocks to find out how many of those equal one of the heavier blocks. Let the children take turns using the balance to make more discoveries about the relative weights of different kinds of table blocks.

Homemade Blocks

Blocks From the Cupboard

Set out a collection of unopened cans of food (leave the labels on). Try to include as many different shapes and sizes as possible, such as tuna fish cans, large and small soup cans, single-serving fruit and vegetable cans, and family-size baked bean cans. Let your children experiment building with the cans. Encourage them to try making a pattern with the cans as they build.

Can Pyramid

Collect six unopened food cans that are exactly the same size. As your children watch, stack the cans in a pyramid with three cans on the bottom row, two on the next row, and one on the top row. Take down the pyramid. Let each child try making the pyramid on his or her own.

Empty Food Box Blocks

Use empty food boxes, such as cookie, cracker, and cereal boxes, to make blocks. Stuff the empty boxes with newspaper and tape the ends closed. Leave the boxes as is or cover them with construction paper, gift-wrap, or brightly colored self-stick paper. Let your children use these lightweight blocks to create walls, roads, towers, and other structures.

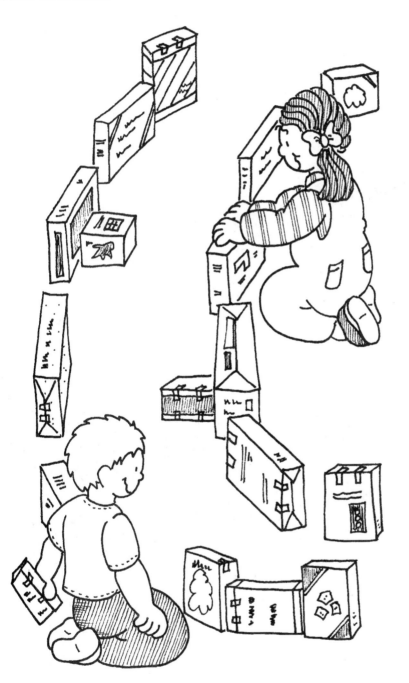

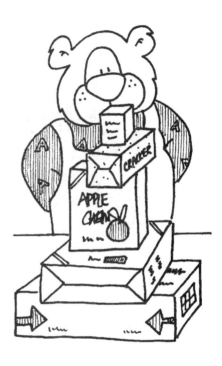

Small to Large

Select four or five Food Box Blocks of varying sizes. Let your children take turns putting them in order from smallest to largest. Then ask them to build a tower with the blocks. Help them discover that their structures are sturdier when the bigger blocks are on the bottom and the smaller blocks are on top.

Grocery Sack Blocks

Make large, lightweight blocks with grocery sacks. Stuff a brown paper grocery sack with crumpled newspaper and tape the top down to create a rectangular block shape. Make as many of these blocks as you wish. Give the blocks to your children and let them discover new structures they can build. Let the children take the blocks outside for a different kind of building experience.

All Together Now

Give each of your children a brown paper grocery sack. Have the children decorate their sacks with crayons or felt tip markers. Turn each child's grocery sack into a block by following the directions on this page. Give each child his or her Grocery Sack Block. Ask the children to think of all the things they can do with their one block. They will probably think of a few things, but not many. Now have them name all the things they can do if they put their blocks together. Let them try some of their ideas. Point out how sharing their blocks is much more fun and interesting.

Milk Carton Blocks

Cut the tops off cardboard milk cartons and discard. Rinse and dry the cartons well. To make each block, you will need two cartons the same size (two half-gallon, two quart, etc.). Fill one of the cartons with crumpled newspaper for extra strength, if you wish. Slide the top of one carton over the top of the other. Tape the outside edges so that the cartons cannot be pulled apart. Make as many blocks as you wish. These blocks are similar to hollow blocks and can be used in many of the same ways. Encourage the children to try building a tower as tall as themselves with these blocks.

How Many Blocks?

Build a structure with some Milk Carton Blocks. Have your children look at the structure and then guess (without counting) how many blocks you used to create it. Now count the blocks together. Were their guesses too high, too low, or just right? Repeat with a different number of blocks, or let the children build a structure and have you guess how many blocks are in it.

Tissue Box Blocks

Collect empty boxes of facial tissue. Be sure to have some long rectangular boxes and some square boxes. Stuff the boxes with crumpled newspaper and tape the openings shut. These blocks are fun because the tissue boxes have interesting designs. Let your children explore building colorful walls and towers with these blocks.

Tower Game

Set out rectangular and square Tissue Box Blocks. Have your children sort them by size. Then let them estimate which would be taller, a tower made from five square blocks or a tower made from five rectangular blocks. Have them build the two towers to check their guess. Repeat with other combinations. For example, which is taller, a tower made of two square blocks and two rectangular blocks or a tower made of three rectangular blocks? Or, which is shorter, a tower of four rectangular blocks or a tower of eight square blocks?

Ice Blocks

Cut cardboard milk cartons in half and discard the top half. Fill the cartons with water and freeze them. (If you wish, add food coloring to the water before freezing it.) Fill several ice cube trays with water and freeze them too. Set large waterproof trays on a table and place the ice "blocks" on them. Show your children how to put these blocks together by shaking a little salt on one block and placing another Ice Block on top of the salt. (The salt makes the Ice Blocks freeze together.) Let the children make ice sculptures with these temporary blocks.

Melting Blocks

After your children have finished building with the Ice Blocks, take photographs of the sculptors and their sculptures to use in making a collage or a block book. Then have the children select places for their trays of ice sculptures to melt. (Be sure that the trays are deep enough to hold all of the melted water.) Have them think about where in the room the ice would melt the fastest and where it would melt the slowest. Let them place their ice sculptures around the room and monitor the melting ice throughout the day.

Picture Blocks

To make a collection of Picture Blocks for your children, tape the ends of small, square cardboard boxes securely closed. (Square gift boxes or square facial tissue boxes work well for this.) Glue colorful pictures or photographs to the sides of the boxes. Cover the boxes with clear self-stick paper for durability. Encourage the children to incorporate the pictures on the blocks into their block play.

Matching Pictures

When making the Picture Blocks on this page, select pairs of pictures to put on them. Glue the pictures to the blocks, making sure that each half of a pair is on a different block. Set out the blocks and let your children take turns finding the matching pictures.

Spool Blocks

Collect a variety of empty wooden or plastic thread spools. (Wooden spools can be purchased at craft stores.) Put the spools in a basket or a bin. Let your children experiment building with the spools. How many spools can they stack to make a tower? What is the easiest way to build a wall with the spools? Help them notice the different sizes of spools and how the size affects their building.

Spool Trees

Collect six spools for each of your children. Have the children arrange their spools in a pyramid shape with three spools on the bottom, two in the middle, and one on the top. Help them glue their spools in place. When the glue has dried, let the children paint their spools green to turn them into "trees."

Sponge Blocks

Collect a variety of colors of thick synthetic sponges. Cut the sponges into identical square shapes. Let your children use these Sponge Blocks to create lightweight sculptures. Is it easier or harder to stack them than regular wooden blocks? What is the highest tower they can make with the Sponge Blocks?

Fun With Many Blocks

Put out an assortment of three or four kinds of table blocks, including Sponge Blocks. Invite your children to create structures using all of the different blocks. Encourage them to discover what blocks work best on the bottom, in the middle, and on the top. Challenge the children to create a pattern with the different blocks as they build.

Container Blocks

Plastic containers of all sorts can make interesting building blocks. Collect several containers that nest together. Show your children how to build a tower with them by turning the largest container upside down on a flat surface, selecting the next largest container, and placing it upside down on the first one. Repeat, until you have used all of the containers. Take the tower apart and let your children try to make it.

Pyramid of Cups

Collect as many empty yogurt cups of one size as possible. Let your children create a giant pyramid out of the cups. How many stories high can they build it? Continue adding identical yogurt cups to the collection to make the pyramid as tall as possible.

Plastic Ring Blocks

Save empty 2-liter plastic bottles. Cut the top and bottom off of each bottle, then cut the center section into 3-inch lengths. Smooth off any rough edges. Let your children build walls and pyramids with these rings.

Guessing Game

Set out an object, such as a large toy car or a basket. Have your children guess how many Plastic Ring Blocks it will take to make a complete circle around the object. Let them use the Plastic Ring Blocks to make a circle around the object. Help them count the total number of blocks in the circle. How does this number compare to the number they guessed? Let them try this with other objects of different sizes.

Pillow Blocks

Collect pillows of all sizes and shapes. Invite your children to bring in a variety of pillows to leave in your room for a while. Keep the pillows in a large box or a small inflatable swimming pool. Let your children use the pillows as blocks. Challenge them to build a wall with the pillows. How many pillows can they stack? Encourage them to think of new and different ways to use their Pillow Blocks.

Pillow House

Talk with your children about ways they could use the Pillow Blocks to make the outline of a house. Ask them to tell you what kinds of rooms their house would have. Then let them use the Pillow Blocks to create their house. Let them bring props from other parts of the classroom to add to their "pillow house."

Cube Blocks

Using the pattern on page 77 as a guide, cut Cube Block pattern shapes out of sturdy paper. Fold each pattern shape into a cube, following the illustrations on this page. Tape the edges closed. Make a variety of these blocks. If you wish, let your children decorate the pattern shapes before you fold them. Or, enlarge or reduce the pattern to make different sizes of Cube Blocks. When the Cube Blocks are completed, let the children experiment building and creating with them.

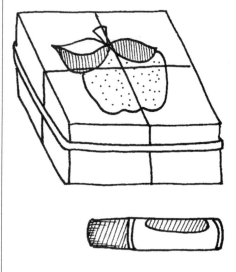

Puzzle Blocks

Put four Cube Blocks together in a square shape and hold them in place with a rubber band. Draw a simple picture across the top of all four blocks. Turn each block so that a blank side is on the top. Secure all of the blocks with the rubber band and draw a different picture across all four blocks. Repeat four more times until each side of each block has a part of a picture drawn on it. Give the Puzzle Blocks to your children. Let them put the blocks together so that a complete picture is showing on the top. Encourage them to find all six puzzles.

Cube Block Pattern

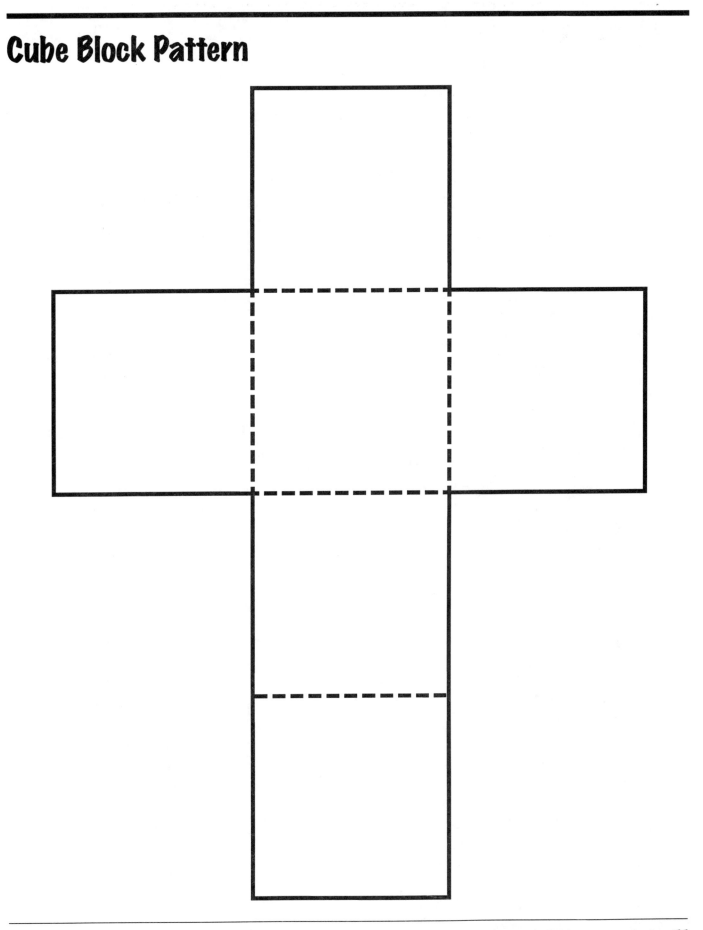

Totline® Publications

Early Learning Resources

Songs, activities, themes, recipes, and tips

Celebrations

Easy, practical ideas for celebrating holidays and special days around the world. Plus ideas for making ordinary days special.

Celebrating Likes and Differences
Small World Celebrations
Special Day Celebrations
Great Big Holiday Celebrations

Theme-A-Saurus®

Classroom-tested, around-the-curriculum activities organized into imaginative units. Great for implementing child-directed programs.

Multisensory Theme-A-Saurus
Theme-A-Saurus
Theme-A-Saurus II
Toddler Theme-A-Saurus
Alphabet Theme-A-Saurus
Nursery Rhyme Theme-A-Saurus
Storytime Theme-A-Saurus

1•2•3 Series

Open-ended, age-appropriate, cooperative, and no-lose experiences for working with preschool children.

1•2•3 Art
1•2•3 Games
1•2•3 Colors
1•2•3 Puppets
1•2•3 Reading & Writing
1•2•3 Rhymes, Stories & Songs
1•2•3 Math
1•2•3 Science
1•2•3 Shapes

Snacks Series

Easy, educational recipes for healthy eating and expanded learning.

Super Snacks
Healthy Snacks
Teaching Snacks
Multicultural Snacks

Piggyback® Songs

New songs sung to the tunes of childhood favorites. No music to read! Easy for adults and children to learn. Chorded for guitar or autoharp.

Piggyback Songs
More Piggyback Songs
Piggyback Songs for Infants & Toddlers
Piggyback Songs in Praise of God
Piggyback Songs in Praise of Jesus
Holiday Piggyback Songs
Animal Piggyback Songs
Piggyback Songs for School
Piggyback Songs to Sign
Spanish Piggyback Songs
More Piggyback Songs for School

Busy Bees

These seasonal books help two- and three-year-olds discover the world around them through their senses. Each book includes fun activity and learning ideas, songs, snack ideas, and more!

Busy Bees—SPRING
Busy Bees—SUMMER
Busy Bees—FALL
Busy Bees—WINTER

101 Tips for Directors

Great ideas for managing a preschool or daycare. These hassle-free, handy hints are a great help.

Staff and Parent Self-Esteem
Parent Communication
Health and Safety
Marketing Your Center
Resources for You and Your Center
Child Development Training

101 Tips for Toddler Teachers

Designed for adults who work with toddlers.

Classroom Management
Discovery Play
Dramatic Play
Large Motor Play
Small Motor Play
Word Play

101 Tips for Preschool Teachers

Valuable, fresh ideas for adults who work with young children.

Creating Theme Environments
Encouraging Creativity
Developing Motor Skills
Developing Language Skills
Teaching Basic Concepts
Spicing Up Learning Centers

Problem Solving Safari

Designed to help children problem-solve and think for themselves. Each book includes scenarios from children's real play and possible solutions.

Problem Solving Safari—Art
Problem Solving Safari—Blocks
Problem Solving Safari—Dramatic Play
Problem Solving Safari—Manipulatives
Problem Solving Safari—Outdoors
Problem Solving Safari—Science

The Best of Totline® Series

Collections of some of the finest, most useful material published in *Totline Magazine* over the years.

The Best of Totline
The Best of Totline Parent Flyers

Early Learning Resources

Posters, puzzles, and books for parents and children

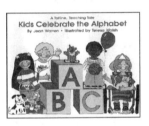

A Year of Fun

Age-specific books detailing how young children grow and change and what parents can do to lay a foundation for later learning.

Just for Babies
Just for Ones
Just for Twos
Just for Threes
Just for Fours
Just for Fives

Getting Ready for School

Fun, easy-to-follow ideas for developing essential skills that preschoolers need before they can successfully achieve higher levels of learning.

Ready to Learn Colors, Shapes, and Numbers
Ready to Write and Develop Motor Skills
Ready to Read
Ready to Communicate
Ready to Listen and Explore the Senses

Learning Everywhere

Everyday opportunities for teaching children about language, art, science, math, problem solving, self-esteem, and more!

Teaching House
Teaching Town
Teaching Trips

Beginning Fun With Art

Introduce young children to the fun of art while developing coordination skills and building self-confidence.

Craft Sticks • Crayons • Felt
Glue • Paint • Paper Shapes
Modeling Dough • Yarn
Tissue Paper • Scissors
Rubber Stamps • Stickers

Beginning Fun With Science

Make science fun with these quick, safe, easy-to-do activities that lead to discovery and spark the imagination.

Bugs & Butterflies
Plants & Flowers
Magnets
Rainbows & Colors
Sand & Shells
Water & Bubbles

Teaching Tales

Each of these children's books includes a delightful story plus related activity ideas that expand on the story's theme.

Kids Celebrate the Alphabet
Kids Celebrate Numbers

Seeds for Success™

For parents who want to plant the seeds for success in their young children

Growing Creative Kids
Growing Happy Kids
Growing Responsible Kids
Growing Thinking Kids

Learn With Piggyback® Songs

BOOKS AND TAPES
Age-appropriate songs that help children learn!

Songs & Games for Babies
Songs & Games for Toddlers
Songs & Games for Threes
Songs & Games for Fours

Learning Puzzles

Designed to challenge as children grow.

Kids Celebrate Numbers
Kids Celebrate the Alphabet
Bear Hugs 4-in-1 Puzzle Set
Busy Bees 4-in-1 Puzzle Set

Two-Sided Circle Puzzles

Double-sided, giant floor puzzles designed in a circle with cutout pieces for extra learning and fun.

Underwater Adventure
African Adventure

We Work & Play Together Posters

A colorful collection of cuddly bear posters showing adult and children bears playing and working together.

We Build Together
We Cook Together
We Play Together
We Read Together
We Sing Together
We Work Together

Bear Hugs® Health Posters

Encourage young children to develop good health habits. Additional learning activities on back!

We Brush Our Teeth
We Can Exercise
We Cover our Coughs and Sneezes
We Eat Good Food
We Get Our Rest
We Wash Our Hands

Reminder Posters

Photographic examples of children following the rules.

I cover my coughs
I listen quietly
I pick up my toys
I put my things away
I say please and thank you
I share
I use words when I am angry
I wash my hands
I wipe my nose